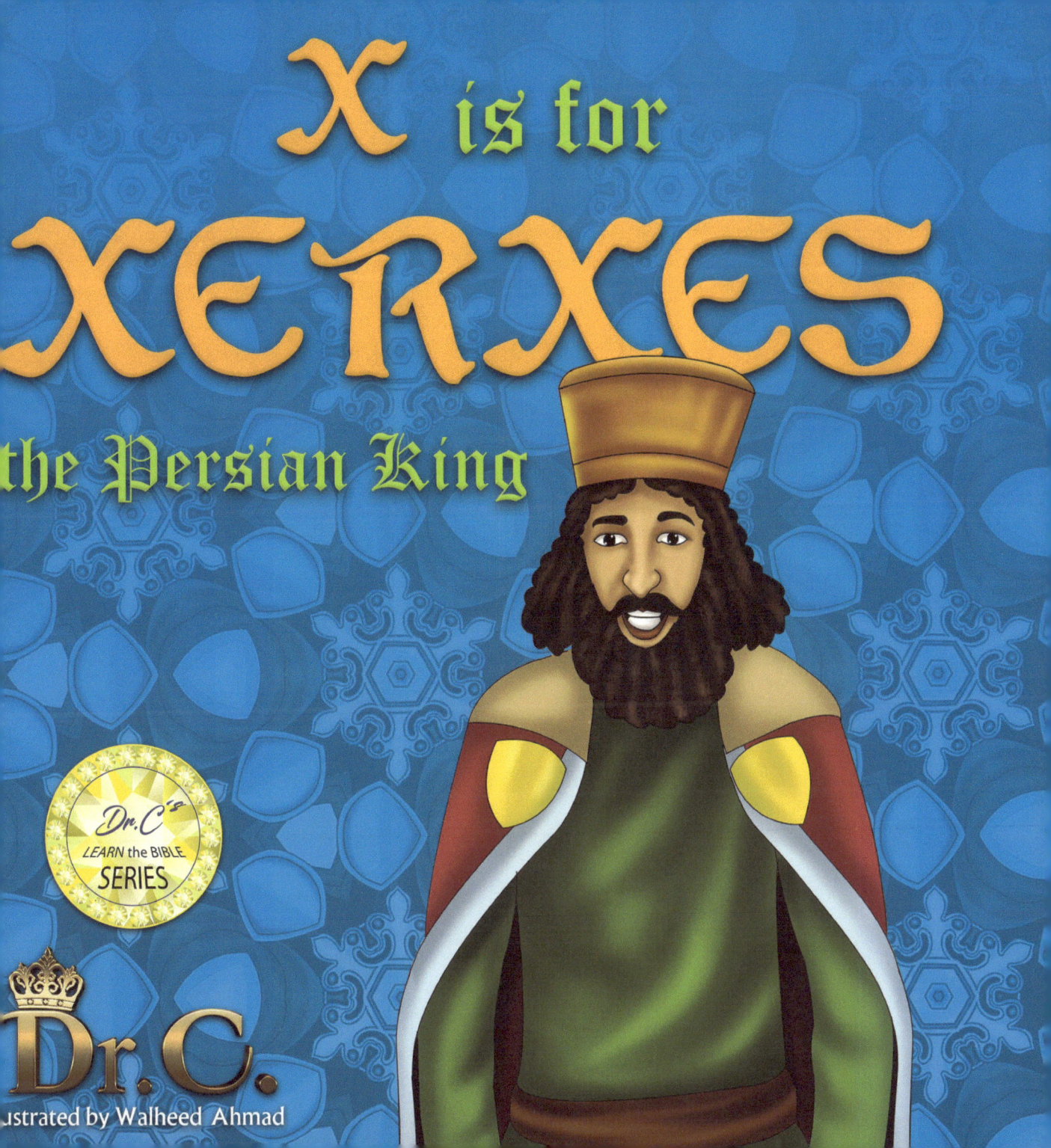

www.clfpublishing.org
909.315.3161

Copyright © 2022 by Cassundra White-Elliott.

All rights reserved. No portion of this book may be reproduced, stored in a retrieval system, or transmitted by any form or any means electronically, photocopied, recorded, or any other except for brief quotations in printed reviews, without the prior permission of the publisher.

Cover design by Senir Design. Contact info: info@senirdesign.com

Illustrations by Walheed Ahmad on Fivver.com.

ISBN #978-1-945102-84-4

Printed in the United States of America.

**Dedicated to**

**All God's Precious Angels**

*"Be kind and compassionate to one another, forgiving each other, just as in Christ God forgave you."*

Ephesians 4:32 (NIV)

Even in situations we do not understand, we should find compassion in our heart for the struggles others endure. Then, our compassion should lead us to finding a way to help when we can.

In this story, a king looked outside of himself into the needs of others, and he acted on their behalf.

In a kingdom in Persia, King Xerxes wanted a queen to live in the palace with him, so he requested all the young maidens to come the kingdom. He talked to each of them until he found one he really liked. Her name was Esther. King Xerxes gave Esther a crown fit for a queen, and she became his bride.

Everything was going well in the kingdom with King Xerxes and his new bride. But one day, all of that changed when Queen Esther's cousin Mordecai told her about an evil plot to kill all the Jews. The plot was hatched by someone very close to the king, but the king did not know anything about it. Queen Esther's heart sank when she heard the news because she and Mordecai were Jews. That meant whatever happened to the other Jews could happen to them, too. On the other hand, King Xerxes was not. He was Persian, but all of them were living in Persia at the time.

One evening as Queen Esther ate dinner alone in her queen's quarters, she thought about the situation that was brewing. She was deeply saddened, and it bothered her so much, she could barely eat. Queen Esther knew she should alert her husband the king, but she was scared about what he would do if she told him she was a Jew and about what was going to happen to her people if he did not step in and use his authority as king. The lives of the Jews were in danger, but King Xerxes could come to the rescue.

Not too long after that day, Queen Esther finally made up her mind to tell her husband about everything that had taken place. One night, Queen Esther had a banquet for her husband and his right hand man, Haman. After dinner, Queen Esther shared the information she had, which included telling her husband that it was Haman who had devised the evil plot. Horrified by what he had heard, King Xerxes decided to help his wife and her people by allowing them to defend themselves in the battle that would soon take place. Later that night, King Xerxes sat at his desk and wrote another decree to go along with the first one because it could not be changed.

By writing the new decree, King Xerxes demonstrated his love for his wife and showed genuine concern for the Jews. His compassion could help save the Jews from being killed.

Many times people will not get involved with other people's concerns. They tend to stay clear when they believe the situation does not have anything to do with them. The truth is what affects one person will eventually effect others.

Thankfully, King Xerxes did not think the way many people do. He allowed his heart of compassion to guide him.

After the battle took place and the Jews had successfully defended themselves, King Xerxes sat in his chair next to the open window. He could hear the voices of the people as they passed by the palace. Some voices were of Persians and other voices were of Jews. King Xerxes was pleased to hear the voices of all the people that lived in Persia. Although the people had different backgrounds, there was no reason they could not live together in harmony in the same place.

Do you live in harmony with the people who live near you, even if they are from different races or come from different lands? God loves all people regardless of where they were born or where they live now. Remember, Jesus died for all of us.

www.ingramcontent.com/pod-product-compliance
Lightning Source LLC
Chambersburg PA
CBHW041933160426
42813CB00103B/2906